Lighthouses of the Cape

Donella J. Lucero
Nancy L. Hobbs

Lighthouses of the Cape
2009 First Edition
2014 Second Edition
©Willapa Communications

Printed and bound in Canada

ISBN 978-0-615-32993-2

Lucero, Donella J.
Hobbs, Nancy L.

In 2013, North Head lighthouse was transferred from the United States Coast Guard and turned over to Washington State Parks and Recreation Commission.

This book is dedicated to our parents, Don and Gerry Urban who instilled in us a love of history and adventure.

Proper ladies look out toward the Pacific Ocean from Cape Disappointment lighthouse battery. The gun on the left is "Old Betsy" a 15-inch smoothbore Rodman, the largest of the Civil War cannons at Fort Canby (ca. 1870).

Crossing the Bar

Sunset and evening star,
and one clear call for me!
And may there be no moaning of the bar,
when I put out to sea,

But such a tide as moving seems asleep,
too full for sound and foam,
when that which drew from out the boundless deep
turns again home.

Twilight and evening bell,
and after that the dark!
and may there be no sadness of farewell,
when I embark;

For though from out our bourne of Time and Place
the flood may bear me far,
I hope to see my Pilot face to face
when I have crossed the bar.

Alfred Lord Tennyson

Cape Disappointment Lighthouse, Established 1856

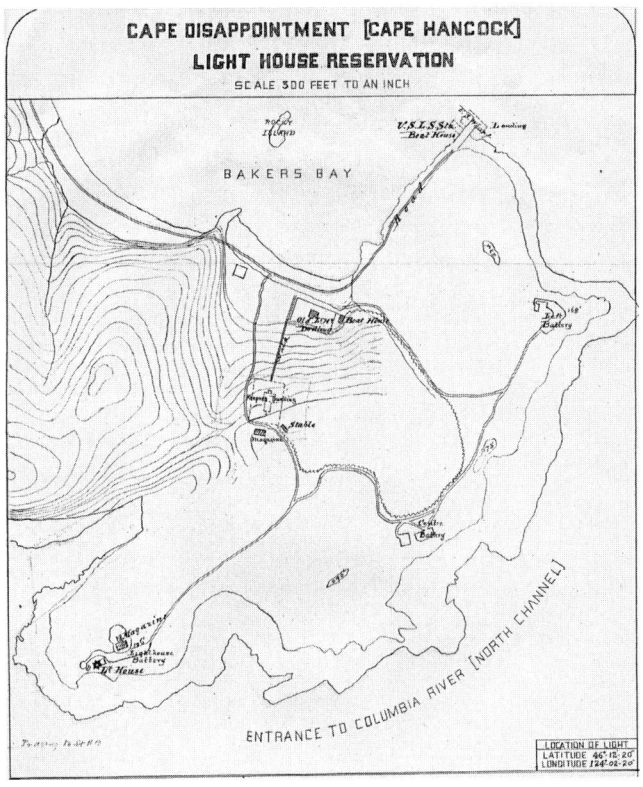

Map of Cape Disappointment Lighthouse Reservation prepared by G.L. Gillespie, Lighthouse Engineer 13th District in December of 1878. The map notes the location of Cape Disappointment light as Latitude 46° 12' 20" and Longitude 124° 02' 20". Labeled are the lighthouse buildings, U.S. Life Saving Service, as well as the three Fort Canby Civil War era gun batteries. (Courtesy, U.S. Coast Guard Museum, 13th District)

History

Construction of Cape Disappointment lighthouse was completed in 1856. The 53-foot tower stands 220 feet above sea level, as a visual landmark for ships that approach the mouth of the Columbia River. The lighthouse was built on a basalt cliff at the most southwest point of Washington state where the river meets the Pacific Ocean.

This headland was first named Kah'eese by the Chinook who lived in the region. Spaniard Bruno de Heceta named it Cape San Roque in 1775. From his ship the *Santiago*, Heceta documented what he thought was a large river. Due to the illness of his crew, he was unable to delay his travel and explore further. It was thirteen years later, in 1788 that British Captain John Meares looked for the river that Heceta noted on his map. Meares arrived at the location, but instead of a river, saw what he thought was the mouth of a wide bay. He named that bay, Deception Bay and the bluff Cape Disappointment. It would be 1792 before American Captain Robert Gray would arrive and discover the river Meares missed. Gray named the river "Columbia" after his ship the *Columbia Rediviva*. He named the bluff on the north side of the river, Cape Hancock. While this still remains the official government name for the site, the bluff continues to be called the more popular name of Cape Disappointment.

In 1846, Lt. William McArthur, Captain of the coast survey vessel *Ewing*, recommended that a lighthouse be built on the southwest slope of the head at Cape Disappointment. He also recommended that it not be made of wood, so the likelihood of it burning would be minimized. Congress authorized the construction of eight lighthouses on the west coast. Cape Disappointment would be one of the eight.

Prior to the building of the lighthouse, mariners would first sail close to Sand Island and use three trimmed spruce trees as a marker to safely cross the bar. Because of the shifting sand, this system was not always successful. The depth and the location of the channel into the river constantly changed. At times it was difficult or even impossible to cross the bar. Many ships went aground in this area near Cape Disappointment, often called the "Graveyard of the Pacific."

The contract for construction of the lighthouses was given to Gibbons and Kelly of Baltimore, Maryland. The bark *Oriole* was loaded with supplies to construct the eight lighthouses. As the ship made its way up the coast of California and Oregon, it dropped off supplies at other lighthouse sites. The ship continued heading north and on September 18, 1853 arrived at the mouth of the Columbia River. The *Oriole* anchored off the bar for eight days waiting for the weather to clear. Finally, the impatient captain made an attempt to enter the river. That decision would be a mistake, for soon the ship struck Middle Sands and began to take on water. The crew and passengers some of whom were laborers on their way to work on construction of the lighthouse, took to the lifeboats. All were safe, but the ship and all the supplies for the Cape Disappointment lighthouse sank to the bottom.

In 1854, the second shipment of building materials arrived. They could finally work toward completing the lighthouse. In 1855, another ship arrived with additional supplies including a 1604 lb. fog bell and a First-order Fresnel lens. A modification would have to be made to the upper portion of the lighthouse to allow for the installation of this larger lens. The original plans were designed for a much smaller lighting system.

A road had been cleared through the brush and trees to the remote site of the new lighthouse. Teams of oxen hauled wagonloads of supplies up the sometimes very muddy hill. Originally the plans were to build a combined lighthouse and residence, but due to the steep terrain, the light keeper's residence had to be constructed down the hill from the tower toward Baker's Bay. The separate keeper's residence was completed in 1854 and enlarged in 1865.

Cape Disappointment Lighthouse Keeper's residence (courtesy of Betty Peterson) ca. 1880

Work on the lighthouse progressed slowly as it was becoming difficult to keep a crew to build the structure. The draw of the gold rush and sudden riches was very strong in comparison to the small wages given for hard labor in such a remote location.

The lighthouse was finally completed, and the whitewashed 53-foot masonry tower gleamed against the darker landscape. On October 15, 1856, first keeper, John Boyd lit the five wicks that brought to life the light at Cape

Disappointment. The lighthouse has been in continual service since that date.

This photo shows the fog bell in front of the small building that housed the striking mechanism. To the left is "Old Betsy," the 15-inch smoothbore Rodman cannon, ca. 1864. (Courtesy, U.S. Coast Guard Museum, 13th District)

Early photograph of Cape Disappointment light showing the original workroom and oil storage. Also shown are the Civil War guns of Fort Canby, ca. 1864.

Several changes and repairs were made to the lighthouse and site during the following years. In 1873, a new oil house was erected replacing the original one built in 1856. The updated oil house is visible in the above photo.

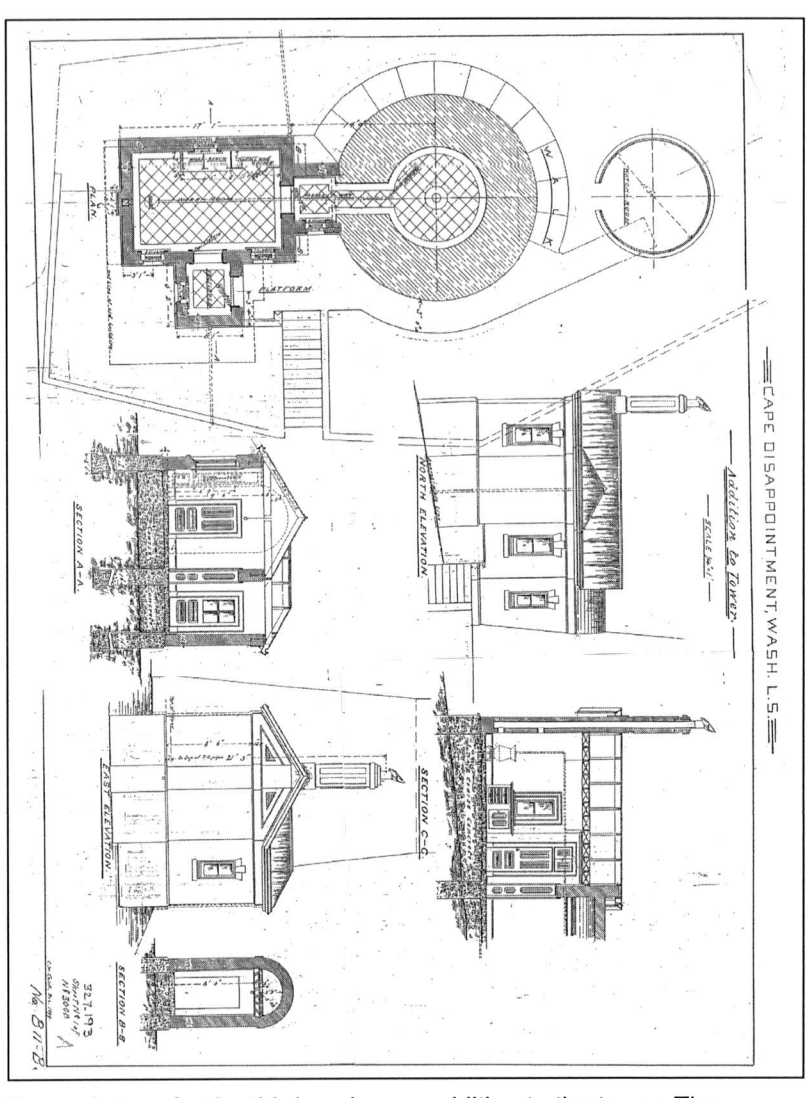

Copy of plans for the third workroom addition to the tower. The plans are dated 1899. The chimney is now gone, but the work-room addition looks much the same today. (Courtesy, U.S. Coast Guard Museum, 13th District).

This photograph ca. 1899 shows the lighthouse very much like it is today. The three keepers are standing in front of the new workroom. (Courtesy, U.S. Coast Guard Museum, 13th District).

The bluff at Cape Disappointment is exposed to storms and harsh weather during the fall and winter months. It has always been a challenge to maintain the lighthouse and site against the elements.

According to the *"Annual Report to the Lighthouse Board"*, a landslide occurred in 1879 that damaged the road leading to the lighthouse and battery. The annual report in 1881 noted, that on January 9th a tornado *"blew down all the fencing and the excessive rainfall at the same time caused the water to flow into the cellars, in such quantities that the floor was covered to a depth of 6-inches, and the small drains were inadequate to carry it off, until great damage had been done to the provisions and supplies stored there. The floors were partly taken up and tile drains put down, which will prevent a like experience in the future."*

Cape Disappointment lighthouse, ca.1898.
(Courtesy, U.S. Coast Guard Museum, 13th District)

In 1896, a concrete retaining wall was installed around the base of the tower and workroom. This replaced the old wooden one. The 1898 annual report states, *"The first order apparatus was removed to North Head light-station and a fourth order illuminating apparatus, showing red and white flashes alternately, having an interval between flashes of fifteen seconds was permanently established here on February 17, 1898."*

The original First-order lens is currently on display at the Lewis and Clark Interpretive Center at Cape Disappointment State Park.

The first-order Fresnel lens installed at Cape Disappointment in 1856 was originally built in France and was the first of two Fresnel lenses used in the United

States. It was originally installed in the south tower of Navesink Lighthouse in New Jersey in 1841. When the twin towers of Navesink fell into disrepair, the lens was transported around Cape Horn to San Francisco to be used in one of the west coast lighthouses planned for construction. After 42 years in Cape Disappointment lighthouse the lens was transferred to North Head in 1898. The lens is 11' 8" high and 6' 5" in diameter. This lens was a fixed lens with a five-wick oil system. Colza oil, whale oil, and eventually kerosene fueled the light.

A fourth-order 1896 Barbier and Benard lens was installed at Cape Disappointment on February 17, 1898 to replace the first-order lens that was moved to North Head lighthouse, two miles to the north. Although not currently in use, the lens is still in the lighthouse.

According to orders, the lighthouse keepers were required to maintain and paint following the *"Instructions to Light-Keepers and Masters of Light-House Vessels"*. These instructions were meant to standardize how lighthouses were operated and maintained. According to this manual the keepers would have been required to whitewash the exterior of the tower and paint any wooden structures dark red, brown, or white. The lanterns and gallery railings were required to be black. Cape Disappointment lighthouse in the past had a solid white tower. It was not until 1972 that a black stripe was painted to distinguish it from North Head.

According to the U.S. Coast Guard, in the early part of World War II the Commandant of the 13th Naval District ordered all lighthouses to be painted in such a way as to conceal it from the water. The disguise was accomplished by using gray and black paint and modifying the outlines of the silhouette. This order was issued to Cape Disappointment lighthouse due to its proximity to Fort Canby.

Cape Disappointment Fog Bell

In 1856, Cape Disappointment lighthouse was put into service. From the beginning, the lighthouse was equipped with a fog bell and wind-up striking apparatus. The 1604 lb. bronze fog bell was cast in Philadelphia, Pennsylvania in 1855 and shipped to Cape Disappointment with the final shipment of building supplies. The first shipment of supplies including a fog bell and lens were transported to the site by the "*Oriole*", they sank along with the ship in 1853, after crossing the Columbia River bar in a storm.

The fog bell and striking mechanism were originally mounted in a building on the northwest side of the lighthouse.

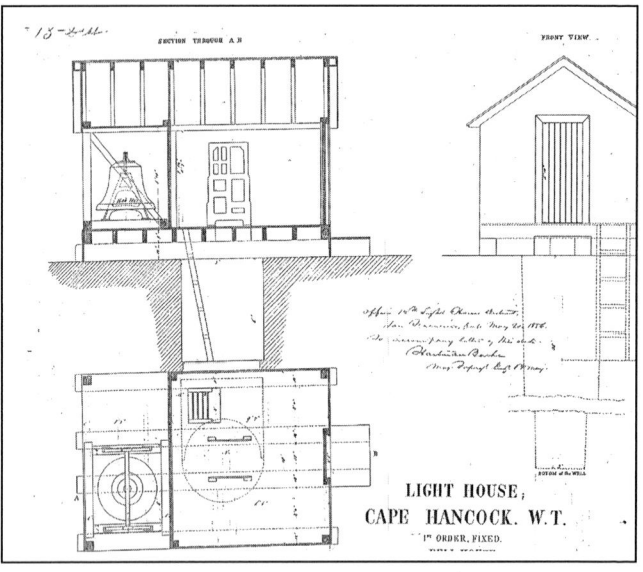

Original fog bell house built in 1856. The plans also indicate a well under the floor. (Courtesy of 13th District U. S. Coast Guard Museum)

According to lighthouse records, *"in July of 1871, the frame of the fog bell was shattered by a blast from a gun from a neighboring battery."* That battery was probably Fort Canby's West Battery also called Lighthouse Battery, the closest one to the lighthouse and bell housing. A new building and frame for the bell was built in August of that same year. It was rebuilt on the southwest side of the lighthouse away from the gun.

On foggy days, the bell would be struck by the hammer of the Steven's fog bell apparatus, sounding a warning to ships coming into the river. Over the years, mariners would complain that the bell could not be heard for any distance. This was blamed on the configuration of the basalt cliffs of the Cape. Due to the inability of the sound to carry far beyond the Cape, the fog bell was moved to another site. According to a report from the Lighthouse Board, *"The fog bell was discontinued July 12, 1881, and transferred to West Point light station, Admiralty Inlet, Puget Sound."*

The bell was transferred again in 1889 to Warrior Rock light station in the Columbia River. In 1969, a barge struck the light, and while the bell was being removed, it was damaged. The original Cape Disappointment fog bell currently sits near the back stairs of the Columbia County Courthouse in St. Helens, Oregon.

Old Betsy and Cape D Lighthouse

Old Betsy was a 15-inch smoothbore Rodman gun, mounted on the west side of the lighthouse during the Civil War era. "Old Betsy," along with two eight-inch guns and four ten-inch guns made up what was called West or Lighthouse Battery at Fort Canby.

According to military records, the gun was fired four times when the U.S. War Department ordered, *"It should not be fired again, because when pointed in certain directions it endangers the glass in the lighthouse."* During at least one practice firing of the gun the concussion broke the glass in the lighthouse. On complaint of the keeper, action was finally taken by the War Department. In 1893, "Old Betsy" was moved to Center Battery, where it could be fired without damage to the lighthouse.

"Old Betsy" shown in front of the fog bell house, ca. 1872'.
(Courtesy, Washington State Parks and Recreation Commission)

Lighthouse Keepers of Cape Disappointment

According the Lighthouse Service records dated 1854 through 1894; the first keeper for the lighthouse at Cape Disappointment was John Boyd. He was appointed on November 15, 1854. It would be almost two years before the building of the lighthouse was completed.

On October 15, 1856, Head Keeper Boyd was able to finally light up the Cape Disappointment light to begin its life saving service at the mouth of the Columbia River. After completion of the lighthouse, the first and second assistant keepers B. Lavery and Joseph C. Clark were hired on November 26, 1856. John Boyd served as head keeper until he died in September of 1865.

He was replaced by Joel Munson on October 26, 1865

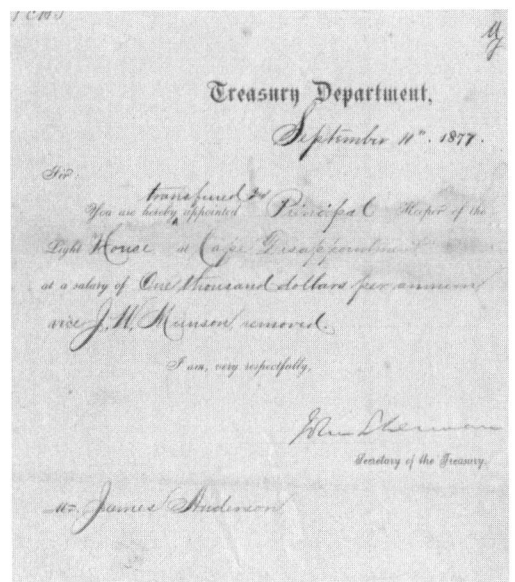

1877 certificate appointing James Anderson as head keeper replacing Joel Munson.

First-order lights were required to have a head keeper and two assistants to manage the light. According *to "The Modern Light-House Service"*, *"the appointment of light-house keepers is restricted to persons between the ages of 18 and 50, who can read, write, and keep accounts, are able to do the requisite manual labor, to pull and sail a boat, and have enough mechanical ability to make the necessary minor repairs about the premises, and keep them painted, whitewashed, and in order."* In remote locations such as Cape Disappointment it was not always possible to hire people who met all of the requirements, especially in the case of the assistant keepers. This same document also stated *"keepers are furnished with quarters for themselves, and in certain cases for their families, when so far distant from market as to make its carriage equal or exceed its cost, with fuel and rations."*

The Keeper's house was located down the hill from the lighthouse towards Baker's Bay on the more sheltered side of the Cape. The main house was divided as a duplex where the head keeper and his family and the 2nd keeper lived. An addition in the back provided housing for the 3rd keeper. Along with the residence was a barn/stable and outbuildings.

According to Lighthouse records written by John Boyd in May of 1865 during an addition to the keeper's house, *"I dislike to make complaints about the assistants, but I think you will not blame me under the circumstances. Mr. Wheeler, a carpenter is here to commence building the addition to the dwelling. He wanted the assistants to dig the postholes to lay the foundation. C. Flores went to the work, but Henry Brown flatly refused. I told him to bring up the lumber, which was landed yesterday and he said it was not his work. This was not his first refusal of duty and he has been very disrespectful since he came here…he says he is ready to leave at any time. Anderson, the man I first engaged, has requested me to take him the first vacancy."* James Anderson was hired to replace Brown just prior to Boyd's death in September of 1865.

Lighthouse keeper, James Anderson. Head keeper from 1877-1894. (Courtesy, Betty Peterson)

Keepers continued to maintain and care for the light until all lighthouse duties were turned over to the U.S. Coast Guard in 1939. Many keepers continued their jobs as members of the Coast Guard.

This was the path the keepers traveled each way between the lighthouse and the keeper's residence down the hill. The current road to the lighthouse is located in this same area. (Courtesy: Washington State Parks & Recreation Commission).

Lighthouse keeper's residence and stable/barn on east side of Cape Disappointment lighthouse. (Courtesy: Washington State Parks & Recreation Commission).

North Head Lighthouse
Established 1898

No 18 NORTH HEAD LIGHT HOUSE WASHINGTON.

History

North Head Lighthouse ca. 1951. (U.S. Coast Guard Museum, 13th District).

   North Head lighthouse shines its light from a basalt bluff 194 feet above the ocean. This point of land is among the foggiest and windiest places on the west coast of the United States. North Head has also been the site of a U.S. Weather station, a wireless signal station, and part of old Fort Canby.
   The lighthouse was built to provide an aid to navigation for ships approaching from the north. In this dangerous area, mariners could not see Cape Disappointment lighthouse, two miles to the south, in time to safely enter the Columbia River channel.

North Head Lighthouse construction ca. 1898. (Washington State Parks and Recreation Commission).

Construction began on North Head lighthouse in 1897. The lighthouse was engineered by German-born C.W. Leick and constructed by George Langford, an early contractor and builder from Portland, Oregon. The tower was built 65 feet above the ground and designed large enough to hold the First-order Fresnel lens transferred from Cape Disappointment lighthouse.

Written in the "Report of the Light-house Board for 1898, *"The contractors furnishing the metal work delivered it on August 15, 1897, 173 days after the expiration of the time for the completion of their contract, incurring a penalty for delay of $4,325, or $160 in excess of the amount they were to receive under the contract."* The government granted the contractor an extension until November 15, 1897. The station was finally completed on April 10, 1898. The next month, on May 16, 1898 it was lit and officially went into service.

At the same time the lighthouse was being constructed, construction workers built two oil houses just to the east of the lighthouse. A keeper's residence, a duplex to house two assistant keepers, a barn, chicken coop and outbuildings were also built around that same time. All of the original buildings are still located on site.

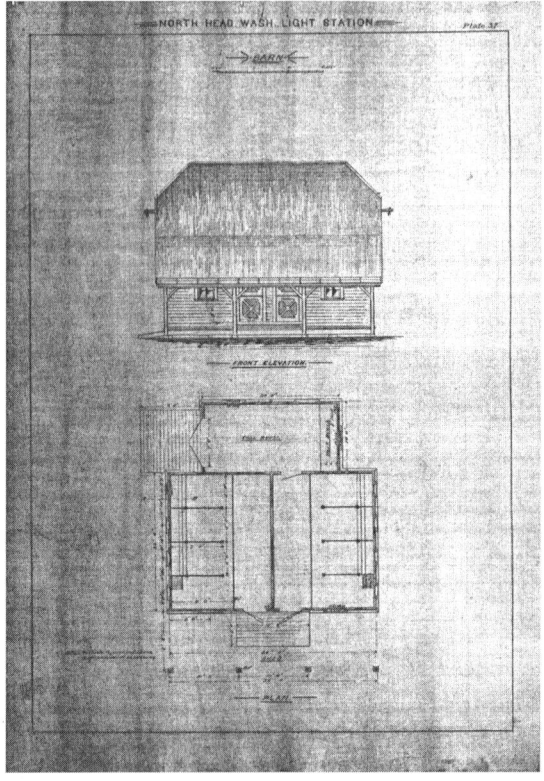

Plans for barn, ca. 1896. The barn had space for six horses or mules, and a tool room including a workbench located in the back of the building. (Washington State Parks and Recreation Commission).

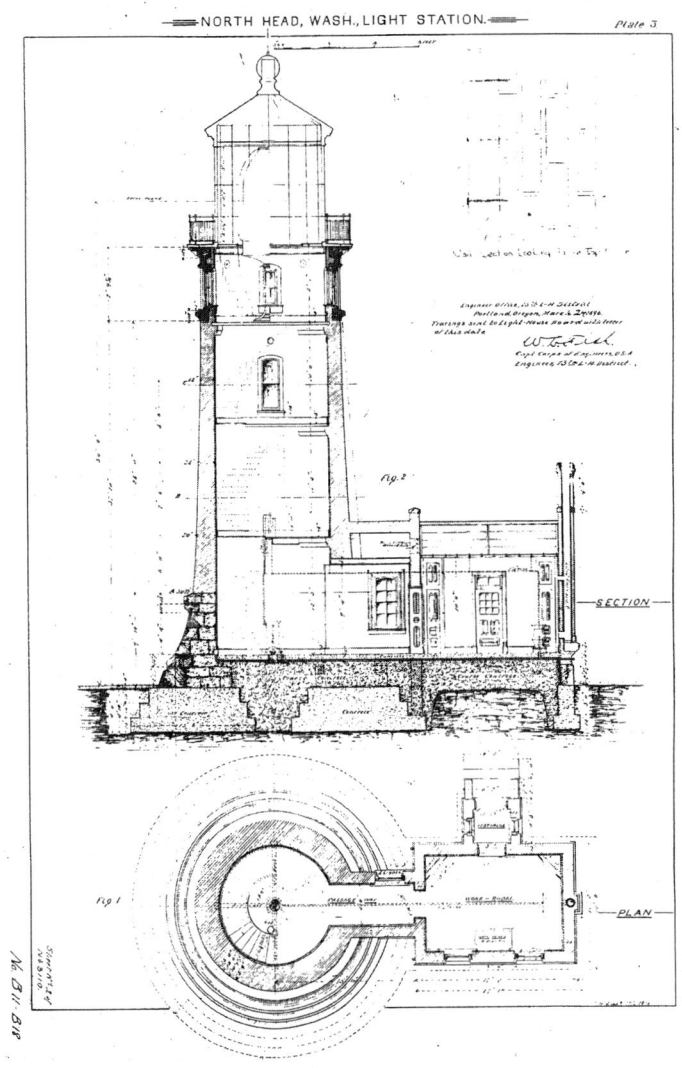

Plans for North Head Lighthouse, ca. 1896. (Washington State Parks and Recreation Commission).

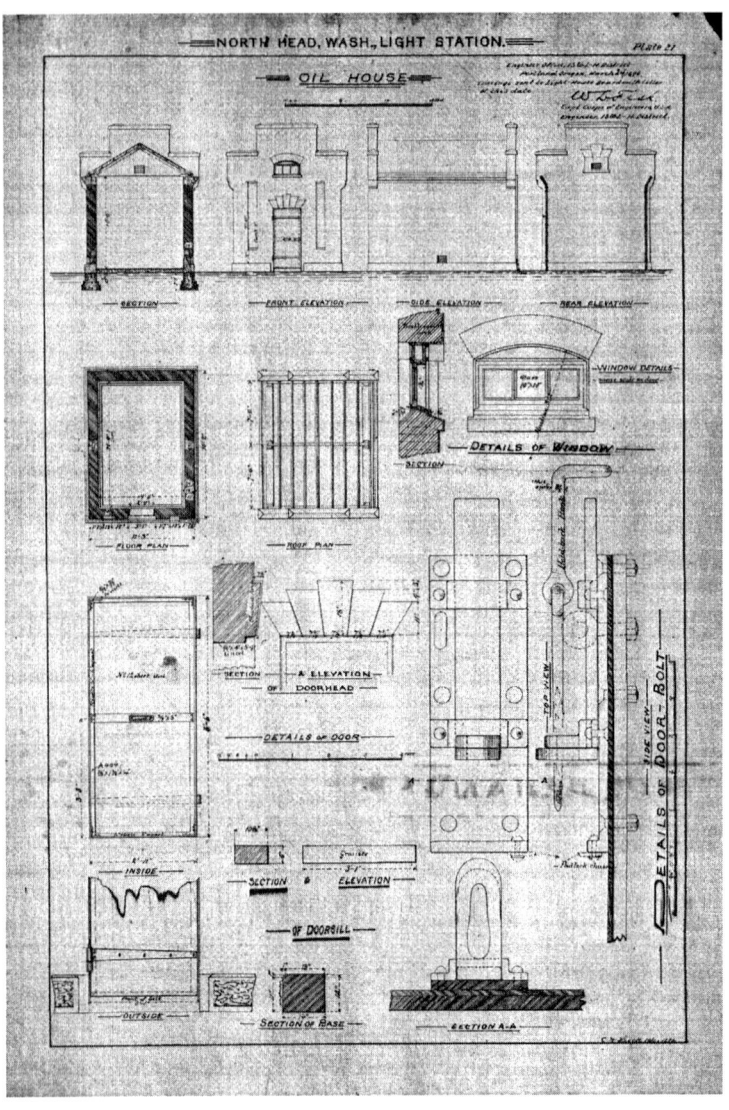

Oil house plans and details, ca.1896. (Washington State Parks and Recreation Commission).

Photograph of North Head lighthouse from the back
fence of the Weather Bureau Station.

The "Light"

The First-order Fresnel lens, installed in 1898 at North Head lighthouse, was built in Paris, France. The lens was shipped to the United States where it was put in service at Navesink lighthouse in New Jersey, until 1852. The lens was then crated and shipped around Cape Horn to San Francisco, California to be used in one of the west coast lighthouses. Because the ship "*Oriole*" sank, while delivering supplies to construct Cape Disappointment lighthouse, it was decided to ship the First-order lens as a replacement for the light system lost in the wreck. The new light was put into service at Cape Disappointment lighthouse on October 15, 1856.

The transfer of the First-order Fresnel lens and five-wick lamp from Cape Disappointment lighthouse to North Head lighthouse occurred in February of 1898. The light was officially lit at North Head on May 16, 1898 by head lighthouse keeper, Alex K. Pesonen.

The light of the First-order Fresnel lens was 80,000 candle power and could be seen 20 miles out to sea. The original cost of the lens was $3,000.-$6,000. Today the value would be well over a million dollars. The large five-wick lamp helped keep the light visible to ships from a long distance. A variety of oils were used to fuel the lamp; colza oil (rape seed oil), whale oil and kerosene were some of the types available in the past.

In 1932, a duck, perhaps blinded by the light, flew toward the lens and broke a window in the North Head lighthouse. The duck also chipped one of the prisms on the lens.

The First-order lens was replaced in 1937 by a rotating double bulls-eye electric powered Fourth-order Fresnel lens. This lens was 260,000 candle power. When the stationary First-order lens was replaced by a rotating lens it was assigned a "signature." The new signature for North Head was *"one second white flash, 6.5 seconds eclipse, one second white flash, 21.5 second eclipse."* (All active lighthouses have a unique signature of flashes and eclipses that allow mariners to identify the specific aide to navigation.)

In 1950, the Fourth-order lens was replaced by 2 revolving semi-automatic lights. The light became fully automated in 1961. Several modifications and upgrades of the lighting system have taken place over time. The current light (2009) is a Marine Rotating Beacon, model VRB-25. Like the First-order Fresnel, it can be seen for 20 miles out to sea.

Records indicate that Cape Disappointment and North Head lights were turned off twice since they were first lit. The first time was a few days after the Japanese bombed Pearl Harbor. On December 10, 1941, orders were issued by the Commandant, 13th Naval District to black out the entire west coast. This order included all lighthouses and navigational aids. Under this order, Cape Disappointment, North Head, the lightship and any lit buoys were shut off. When the ship *"Mauna Ala"* was wrecked on Clatsop Spit because of the black-out, a new order was issued. The lighthouses, lightship and buoys were all re-lit. The second time the lighthouses were shut off was on June 21, 1942 just after Fort Stevens was fired upon by a Japanese submarine. This outage lasted only a few hours.

During World War II, attempts were made to try to hide the very visible lighthouses on the Pacific coast. According to U.S. Coast Guard records,

> *"Early in the war, the Commandant, 13th Naval District ordered the concealment painting of ten of the Light Stations that were near military areas or war industries. The walls were 'toned down' with gray and the space under the eaves painted black to accentuate the silhouette of the Station as it appeared from the water...Army activities near Coast Guard units furnished the paint for camouflaging the structures. The last of the stations was returned to its normal peace time color by the end of the summer, 1945."*

North Head Light

This view shows the lighthouse and oil storage buildings
on the top right. In the lower middle are the keeper and
assistant keeper residences, chicken coop, barn and garages.
This photo was taken after the removal of the weather and
signal stations. (U.S. Coast Guard Museum, 13th District)

This postcard shows the lighthouse keepers relaxing outside North Head lighthouse. The lighthouse had three keepers (one head keeper and two assistants).

North Head Lighthouse Keepers

The first head lighthouse keeper at North Head was Alex K. Pesonen. He was placed in charge of North Head lighthouse on May 16, 1898, the day the lighthouse was put into service. Keeper Pesonen had at one time served on the lighthouse tender *"Manzanita"* and as an assistant keeper at Tillamook lighthouse. He lived at North Head for 26 years. His wife, Mary lived with him until June 9,1923 when she went over the cliff onto the rocks below. The local paper wrote,

> *"The next morning she arose at five o'clock telling Mr. Pesonen to remain in bed for a while longer. She told him she would also attend to some small errands and would then take a short walk, something her doctor had advised. She left the house and was never seen alive again."*

The keepers little dog, always accompanied his mistress on her walks. This day he came back alone and acted strangely. The newspaper article continued,

> *"He notified the boys at the radio station and also at the weather bureau and a searching party was soon organized. The dog lead searchers to a spot just under the fire control station near the North head lighthouse and there they found her coat lying on the edge of the cliff. A trail through the tall grass as though someone had slid down the cliff was mute evidence of what had befallen the unfortunate woman...searching parties were immediately organized in an effort to find the body. Blasting was resorted to but nothing came of it, until about five*

*o'clock in the evening, when Frank Hammond one
of the assistant keepers found the body lying in a
little cove just beyond the Pesonen garden, where
it had drifted with the tide."*

It will never be known if Mary's death was accident or
suicide but the story is fascinating to many. This sad tale
has sprouted many reports of a female ghost at the
lighthouse.

A.K. Pesonen retired on September 30, 1924 after 26
years of service. He died in 1925 and was buried next to
his wife in the Ilwaco Cemetery.
    During the time Pesonen was head keeper, he had a
second assistant keeper by the name of Mabel E.
Bretherton. She was the only female keeper assigned to
North Head lighthouse. From 1905 until her resignation on
October 31, 1907 she assisted in the care and operation
of the light. Mabel Bretherton had also served at Cape
Blanco lighthouse in Oregon prior to coming to North
Head.
    On A.K. Pesonen's retirement, his second keeper A.J.
"Gus" Siniluto became head keeper. Leonard W. Gabriel
was third assistant keeper under A.K. Pesonen for eight
years and worked as second keeper under Siniluto. He
took over as head lighthouse keeper on the retirement of
Siniluto on March 1, 1937. Gabriel served in this capacity
until his retirement, April 7, 1944.
    Lighthouse keepers and their families had a remote and
hard life. Keepers would traditionally work 8-hour shifts if
there were three keepers. If one of the keepers left, the
hours would become much longer. The light was lit from
dusk to dawn with cleaning and polishing being done

during the daylight hours. The cleaning and maintenance of the light and lens was the most important duty of the keepers.

The keeper's wives were also subject to the regulations of the Lighthouse Service. They were required to do their household duties according to regulations and were also subject to inspection.

Head keepers at North Head would make approximately $800-$1000 per year and would live in the head keeper's residence closest to the lighthouse. The second keeper would make approximately $600 per year and live in half of the duplex. The other side of the duplex was occupied by the third keeper, who made approximately $550 per year. The keeper's rank determined where they lived at North Head and according to records it seemed to determine how many lights were in the dining room chandelier. The head keeper's house had 6 lights, the second keeper's residence had 5 and the third keeper's residence had 4 lights.

Lighthouse Keeper dwelling plans, ca. 1896. (Washington State Parks and Recreation Commission).

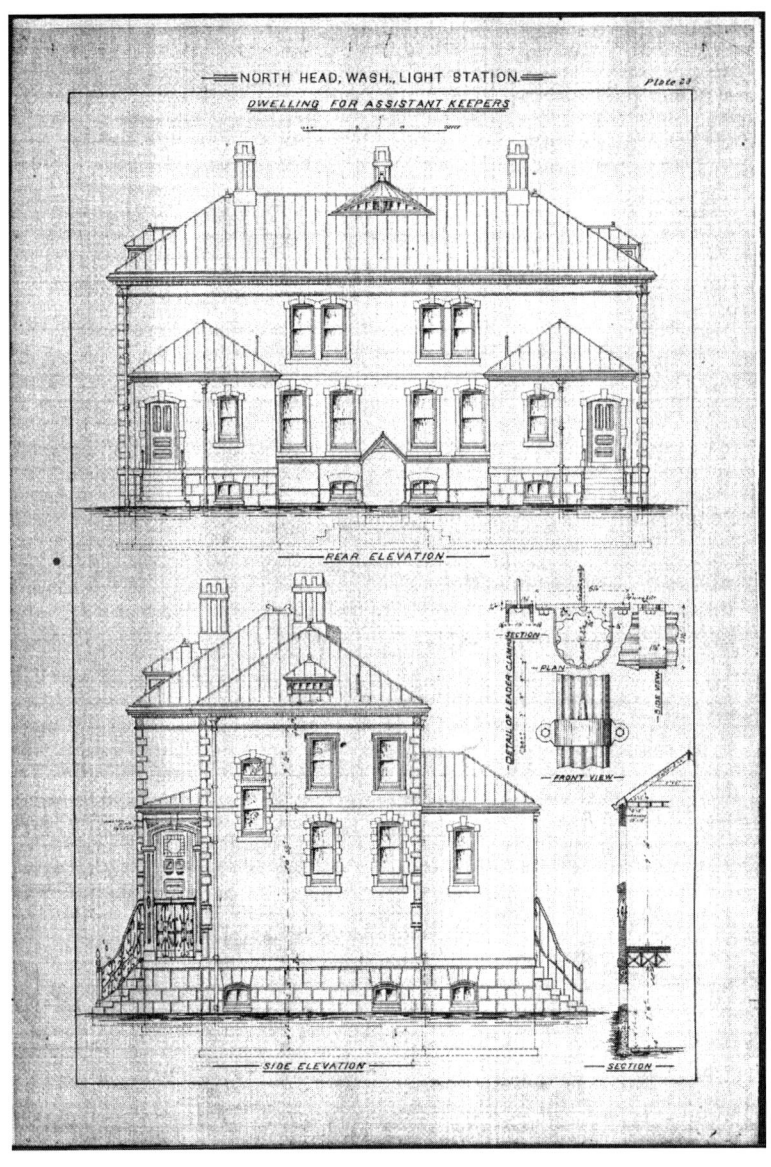

Assistant Keepers duplex dwelling plans, ca.1896. (Washington State Parks and Recreation Commission).

North Head Lighthouse Road

NO.3.3 DRIVE NORTH HEAD LIGHT HOUSE NORTH BEACH WASHINGTON.

   Access to North Head lighthouse from Ilwaco was by the lighthouse plank road. This road was especially bumpy and was repaired by using pieces of shipwrecks to patch any holes. The plank road remained until it was graveled in the1930's.

Waiting for the Fleet, North Head, Wash.

Watching the Great White Fleet

The "Great White Fleet" or Atlantic Fleet was a contingent of sixteen battleships sent by Teddy Roosevelt around the world in December of 1907. All of the battleships were painted white except for the bows, which were decorated with gilded scrollwork. The purpose of the world cruise of the "Great White Fleet" was to impress upon the world the greatness of the American Navy. This fleet traveled over 43,000 nautical miles. In May of 1908 the fleet came up the western coast of the United States very much in view of the people of the Long Beach Peninsula.

According to the May 22,1908 Chinook Observer,

"Wednesday was a fair day, and being the day on which the Atlantic Fleet was to pass north in front of the mouth of the Columbia on it's way to Puget Sound. Chinook was nearly depopulated from early morning until 3:30 pm. All the fish launchers belonging to the Bakers Bay Trap men were donated by their owners to any and all the people of Chinook for a free trip to Ft. Canby, to give the privilege of witnessing the most imposing Naval procession that ever appeared in the North Pacific. The result was that all that could spare the time accepted the invitation and there was a string of launches on the way to Canby from 5-8 am. Some went down in wagons. The dock at Ft. Canby was crowded with all kinds of boats, from the largest of the lower river steamers to the smallest sailboat, many of them in gala attire. Before 12 the Ft. Canby light hill, Mackenzie and North Heads were *blacked with people from both sides of the river armed with field glasses and lunch baskets, awaiting the appearance of the fleet. About 10 o'clock it could be seen far below Tillamuk Rock (Tillamook Rock), in a cloud of smoke and later about 12 o'clock it swung into Klatsup Beach (Clatsop Beach), at Seaside, plainly visible through the glasses, sixteen white war ships being in line. At the mouth of the Columbia it slowed down and everybody on the hill had a good view of it, as the distance would permit, which was probably seven miles. The parade of the ships was calm, but the crowd that attended was interesting, and the departure of the mosquito fleet for home, leaving Ft. Canby, with all kinds of water craft loaded with people was the prettiest and liveliest sight of the day. The Chinookers arrived home about 3:30 pm."*

Photo of Great White Fleet passing North Head

This view from the lighthouse toward the east shows the U.S. Weather Bureau Station. The keeper's residences are in the background. (U. S. Coast Guard Museum,13th District).

A view facing west showing the Wireless Signal Station mast. Note the Head Keeper's residence on the left, barn and chicken coop on right. Behind the tower is the U.S. Weather Bureau Station.

Acknowledgements
We would like to acknowledge the following people for their contributions to this book:

Gene Davis of the 13th District U.S. Coast Guard Museum in Seattle. Thank you for your time and patience in helping us locate information and photographs that have helped bring lighthouse history to life.

Betty Peterson who so generously provided photos from her family collection and shared with us some of her family history.

Washington State Parks and Recreation for use of their photographs and research library.

Bibliography

Instructions to Lighthouse Keepers and Masters of Lighthouse Vessels. Washington: Government Printing Office. 1902.

Johnson, Arnold Burges. The Modern Lighthouse Service. Washington: Government Printing Office. 1889.

U.S. Coast Guard History, 13th Naval District. USCG Museum.

U.S. War Department. General Orders. Washington: Government Printing Office. 1893.

Light-House Board Reports 1895-1898.

Lighthouse Service Annual Reports 1854-1894

Chinook Observer 1908 and 1923.

A picturesque photograph of North Head lighthouse and it's two nearby oil houses. ca. 1905 (Washington State Parks and Recreation Commission).